Structural Safety Limits in Catamaran Engine Room Modifications

Dr. Debby R. Lekatompessy

Department of Naval Engineering, Faculty of Engineering,
Pattimura University

ACKNOWLEDGEMENTS

I would like to extend my deepest gratitude to all those who have supported and guided me throughout the completion of this work.

Firstly, my sincere appreciation goes to Pattimura University, especially the Department of Naval Engineering, Faculty of Engineering, for providing the resources and academic environment necessary for the advancement of this research. My heartfelt thanks also go to my mentors and colleagues in the department, whose expertise, encouragement, and insights have greatly enriched my understanding and contributed to the quality of this work.

My gratitude also extends to my family and friends, whose understanding, patience, and encouragement have been a constant source of motivation. Their support has allowed me to persevere during challenging times and celebrate the milestones along the way.

Finally, I would like to thank all my students and colleagues who contributed directly or indirectly to this project. Their curiosity and enthusiasm for naval engineering continue to inspire me and reinforce my commitment to this field.

Thank you all for your invaluable contributions and support. This work would not have been possible without you.

CONTENTS

I INTRODUCTION

1.1 Background of Study

Keywords: Structural modification, catamaran, safety limit

In maritime engineering, structural modifications to existing vessels are a common necessity driven by operational demands and evolving usage needs. Modifications often involve adding new components or increasing load capacities in specific areas of a vessel, such as the engine room. Such alterations, if not supported by appropriate structural reinforcements, can accelerate material fatigue and compromise the vessel's structural integrity. This concern is especially significant in high-speed vessels like catamarans, which rely on lightweight materials, such as aluminum alloys, to maximize performance. However, these materials are also prone to stress limitations when exposed to excessive or poorly distributed loads (Magoga, Aksu, & Slater, 2023).

Catamarans, characterized by their twin-hull design, present unique engineering challenges due to their wide beam and relatively lightweight structure, which makes them susceptible to load-induced stresses. The engine room, as a critical area for load-bearing, particularly requires careful assessment when additional weight is added. Failure to maintain safe stress levels in this section can lead to catastrophic failures, not only risking the vessel's structural stability but also endangering passengers and crew (Hosseinabadi & Khedmati, 2021).

In this context, establishing clear safety limits for structural modifications is essential. Safety limits are defined as the maximum allowable stress or load capacity that a structure can bear without experiencing deformation or structural failure. For aluminum alloy-based catamarans, these limits are particularly crucial because of the material's properties, including high strength-to-weight ratio but relatively low fatigue resistance when subjected to high loads over extended periods (Cheng et al., 2018; Feng et al., 2020). Consequently, it is vital to determine the optimal load thresholds that ensure operational safety while maximizing functional capacity.

The research focuses on defining these safety thresholds through simulation methods and offers an efficient, cost-effective approach. Simulations enable engineers to predict the behavior of structural elements under various load conditions without physical testing, thereby saving both time and resources. By analyzing stress distributions and identifying critical load levels through simulations, engineers can ensure that structural modifications adhere to safety standards. Thus, this study contributes to advancing knowledge on structural limits in marine engineering, particularly for modified catamaran structures, and supports safer, more reliable designs in the maritime industry (Lekatompessy & Zubaydi, 2019).

1.2 Objectives

Keywords: Load safety, engine room, aluminum structure

The primary objective of this study is to determine safe load thresholds for the engine room structure of an aluminum alloy catamaran. Modifications to the vessel, particularly through the addition of passenger space above the engine room, introduce new load-bearing demands that, if not properly assessed, could compromise the structural integrity and safety of the vessel. Identifying and establishing these safe load limits is critical to ensuring the vessel can operate efficiently while maintaining structural safety standards.

Specific Objectives:

1. To Assess Load Safety for Engine Room Modifications: This study aims to evaluate the maximum load that can be safely supported by the engine room deck structure without

exceeding the allowable stress limits of the aluminum alloy material. Understanding load safety is essential in avoiding material fatigue and potential structural failures, particularly in high-speed vessels like catamarans, where lightweight structures are susceptible to stress concentrations under heavy loads (Hosseinabadi & Khcdmati, 2021).

2. To Analyze the Stress Distribution in Aluminum Structures Under Increased Loads: The study employs simulation methods to model the engine room deck under incremental loading conditions, observing how stress is distributed across the structure. Aluminum structures, while advantageous due to their high strength-to-weight ratio, may encounter fatigue more rapidly under excessive stress if safety margins are not properly established. Through simulations, the research aims to map stress responses and identify critical areas where load-induced stresses might exceed safe operational thresholds (Feng et al., 2020).

3. To Define a Safe Load Limit for Engine Room Deck Use in Catamarans:
Based on the simulation results, the study seeks to establish a clear, quantifiable load limit for the engine room deck. This load limit represents the maximum weight the structure can safely bear without requiring additional reinforcement. Such a guideline is essential for ship designers and engineers, providing a benchmark for future modifications or load increases on similar vessels (Lekatompessy & Zubaydi, 2019).

4. To Recommend Structural Reinforcements for Load Exceedance Scenarios: If the load requirements exceed the safe limit identified, the study also aims to propose structural reinforcement strategies, such as increasing the modulus of the cross-sectional area, to accommodate higher loads without compromising safety. Reinforcements would involve modifications to the aluminum alloy structure, ensuring that the vessel maintains its load-bearing capacity while preventing

fatigue or material failure (Cheng et al., 2018).

These objectives support the overarching goal of enhancing maritime safety by establishing scientifically grounded load limits that can be applied to catamaran structures, particularly when considering modifications that increase load demands on specific areas such as the engine room. Achieving these objectives also contributes to more effective structural design practices in the maritime industry, reinforcing safety standards for aluminum-based vessels.

1.3 Research Significance

Keywords: Maritime safety, structural fatigue, cost-effective simulation

The significance of this research lies in its contribution to maritime safety, particularly in ensuring that structural modifications to vessels do not compromise their operational integrity. In maritime engineering, especially with high-speed vessels such as catamarans, safety concerns are paramount as structural fatigue due to excessive or poorly distributed loads can lead to severe operational risks, including structural failure and potential hazards for passengers and crew. By focusing on the structural limits of aluminum alloy catamarans, this study provides critical insights into how modifications and added loads impact safety and longevity in these types of vessels (Magoga, Aksu, & Slater, 2023).

Enhancing Maritime Safety Standards

Maritime safety is a foundational goal of this research. Catamarans, which are often used for passenger transport, tourism, and commercial purposes, must maintain high safety standards to avoid accidents arising from structural issues. The introduction of new load-bearing requirements, such as additional passenger spaces above the engine room, increases the load demands on certain areas of the structure. If these loads exceed the material's stress tolerance, they can induce fatigue and eventually lead to structural compromise. By establishing safe load thresholds, this study contributes to higher safety standards, reducing risks associated with structural fatigue in modified vessels (Hosseinabadi & Khedmati, 2021).

Addressing Structural Fatigue in Aluminum Alloy Vessels

The use of aluminum alloys in ship construction, while advantageous for weight reduction and fuel efficiency, also presents unique challenges. Aluminum has a lower fatigue limit compared to other materials, meaning that without precise load management, the structure may experience faster degradation. This study emphasizes the need for proper load assessments in aluminum alloy vessels, providing guidelines on safe operational loads that prevent premature fatigue. Identifying these limits can help extend the operational life of the vessel, ensuring it remains functional and safe over prolonged use (Feng et al., 2020).

Cost-Effective Simulation for Structural Assessment

One of the major contributions of this research is demonstrating the utility of cost-effective simulation methods in structural assessment. Traditional load testing in maritime engineering can be costly, time-intensive, and may involve risk to the structure itself. By employing simulation, this study offers a method to accurately assess load capacity, stress distribution, and safety limits without physical trials, saving resources while providing reliable data. Simulation has become an increasingly important tool in marine engineering due to its ability to replicate real-world conditions and predict structural behavior under different load scenarios.

The findings of this research underscore the value of simulation for maritime engineers, providing a practical approach for determining safe load thresholds and structural reinforcements (Lekatompessy & Zubaydi, 2019).

In summary, this research addresses three critical areas in maritime engineering: enhancing safety standards, mitigating structural fatigue, and utilizing cost-effective simulation techniques. By setting clear load safety guidelines for modified catamaran structures, particularly in the engine room, this study supports safer and more efficient ship modifications. Furthermore, it provides a framework for the broader maritime industry, demonstrating how simulation-based assessments can be applied to ensure that modified vessels continue to meet safety and performance standards, ultimately benefiting both operators and passengers.

II BACKGROUND AND LITERATURE REVIEW

This chapter provides a comprehensive review of relevant literature and foundational concepts essential for understanding the key aspects of this research. By examining previous studies and theoretical frameworks, the chapter establishes a basis for exploring structural safety limits, load management, and reinforcement strategies in aluminum alloy catamarans. The insights gained from existing research inform the study's approach, highlighting both the achievements and gaps in current maritime engineering practices. This review ensures that the analysis and recommendations presented in subsequent chapters are grounded in well-established knowledge and recent advancements in the field of naval engineering.

2.1 Material Characteristics of Aluminum Alloy in Marine Applications

Keywords: Aluminum alloy, marine materials, tensile strength

Aluminum alloys have gained prominence in marine applications due to their advantageous properties, particularly their high strength-to-weight ratio, corrosion resistance, and ease of fabrication. These characteristics make aluminum alloys suitable for constructing lightweight yet robust marine structures, such as high-speed vessels and catamarans, where minimizing weight without compromising strength is essential. In marine engineering, the use of aluminum alloy reduces fuel consumption, enhances speed, and contributes to the overall efficiency and sustainability of the vessel's operations (Hosseinabadi & Khedmati, 2021).

Strength and Durability

The tensile strength of aluminum alloys is a key factor that contributes to their selection for maritime applications. Tensile strength, defined as the maximum stress an alloy can withstand while being stretched or pulled before breaking, is critical in ensuring that the material can endure the mechanical loads encountered in marine environments. Common aluminum alloys used in marine settings, such as the 5000 and 6000 series, offer high tensile strength combined with excellent resistance to seawater corrosion, a property essential for prolonging the life span of marine vessels operating in saltwater conditions (Hosseinabadi & Khedmati, 2021).

Aluminum alloys also display good fatigue resistance, although they may have lower fatigue limits compared to some other marine materials. This limitation necessitates careful load assessments and structural reinforcements in high-stress areas, particularly in regions subject to cyclic loading. Understanding the fatigue properties of aluminum alloys is essential for engineers when designing components subjected to repetitive forces, such as the hulls of catamarans, where wave impacts and constant loading can lead to material fatigue over time.

Corrosion Resistance and Maintenance Benefits

One of the defining advantages of aluminum alloys in marine applications is their corrosion resistance, particularly against seawater. Aluminum naturally forms a thin oxide layer when exposed to oxygen, which acts as a protective barrier against further corrosion. This property reduces the need for additional coatings or extensive maintenance, making aluminum alloys cost-effective and durable in the long run. In comparison with other materials, such as steel, aluminum's resistance to corrosion translates into lower maintenance costs and enhanced operational reliability in harsh marine environments (Hosseinabadi & Khedmati, 2021).

Formability and Lightweight Construction

Another advantage of aluminum alloys is their formability, allowing for complex structural shapes that can be customized to meet specific design needs in marine engineering. The ductility of aluminum alloys enables them to be molded and welded into various forms, making it possible to achieve intricate designs that contribute to both the aesthetic and functional aspects of modern vessel architecture. This characteristic is especially beneficial for high-speed vessels like catamarans, where aerodynamics and hydrodynamics play a critical role in reducing drag and enhancing fuel efficiency.

Moreover, the lightweight nature of aluminum alloys is essential in the design of vessels that prioritize speed and fuel economy. A lighter vessel requires less power to move, which translates into reduced fuel consumption and emissions, contributing to more sustainable marine operations. This aligns with contemporary environmental goals in maritime engineering, where reducing the carbon footprint of vessels is becoming increasingly important.

The material characteristics of aluminum alloys make them an ideal choice for marine applications, balancing strength, corrosion resistance, and ease of fabrication. However, these benefits come with certain limitations, particularly in fatigue resistance, requiring precise engineering solutions to optimize their performance. Through understanding and leveraging the properties of aluminum alloys, marine engineers can design safer, more efficient vessels that meet the demands of modern maritime operations.

2.2 Structural Modifications and Fatigue Risks

Keywords: Structural modification, fatigue risk, maritime engineering

Structural modifications in marine vessels are often undertaken to improve functionality, enhance capacity, or meet specific operational demands. However, these modifications also introduce additional stresses to the vessel's structure, increasing the risk of fatigue and compromising long-term durability. In maritime engineering, understanding and managing the risks associated with structural modifications are essential, particularly for vessels operating under high-speed or heavy-load conditions. Such changes, if not properly engineered, can accelerate material fatigue and weaken the structure, making it susceptible to cracks, corrosion, and, ultimately, structural failure (Feng et al., 2020).

Impact of Structural Modifications on Fatigue Risks

Fatigue in marine structures is a phenomenon where repeated cyclic stresses lead to the gradual weakening of materials, ultimately causing cracks or fractures. When modifications are made to a vessel—such as adding additional passenger space, equipment, or storage areas—the overall load distribution on the structure changes, leading to new stress points. Over time, these stress concentrations can exacerbate fatigue, particularly in areas already subject to high operational demands, such as the hull or engine room. Modifications that alter the vessel's weight or center of gravity can increase stress on critical components, accelerating fatigue and reducing the vessel's lifespan (Cheng et al., 2018).

The effects of fatigue become more complex when combined with environmental factors, such as exposure to saltwater and wave impacts. The hull and other structural components continuously encounter these forces, leading to what is known as coupled fatigue and corrosion damage. Studies have shown that the ultimate strength of marine structures decreases significantly under combined corrosion and crack damage, which are often aggravated by improper structural modifications (Feng et al., 2020). This makes it essential for engineers to evaluate fatigue risks in modified vessels, incorporating both material characteristics and environmental conditions into their assessments.

Case Studies on Hull Surface and Structural Modifications

Research on hull surface modifications highlights how seemingly minor changes can impact overall vessel performance and structural integrity. For example, modifying the hull surface to optimize hydrodynamic efficiency can alter the stress distribution across the vessel's body. Cheng et al. (2018) demonstrated that such modifications, while beneficial for reducing drag, must be carefully engineered to prevent unintended stress concentrations that could lead to fatigue failures. In high-speed vessels, even slight modifications to the hull design or surface can significantly affect fatigue resistance due to the continuous high-impact forces encountered during operation.

In catamarans and other high-speed vessels, structural modifications often focus on enhancing passenger capacity or increasing storage space, especially above critical areas like the engine room. However, adding weight in these regions without appropriate reinforcement may lead to stress concentrations that exceed the material's fatigue limit, particularly in lightweight aluminum structures. Over time, these stresses can propagate micro-cracks that may not be immediately visible but contribute to gradual weakening and eventual failure under prolonged operational conditions (Feng et al., 2020).

Strategies for Mitigating Fatigue Risks in Structural Modifications

To mitigate fatigue risks associated with structural modifications, engineers must adopt strategies that reinforce high-stress areas and manage load distribution effectively. One approach is to enhance structural stiffness by increasing the cross-sectional modulus of critical components, which allows them to withstand higher loads without excessive deformation. Additionally, incorporating advanced simulation tools during the design phase helps predict stress concentrations and fatigue-prone areas before modifications are implemented. This allows for targeted reinforcements, reducing the likelihood of unexpected fatigue failures.

Moreover, employing high-quality materials and advanced welding techniques can improve joint durability, as the joints are often the first points of fatigue failure in modified structures. By enhancing these areas, engineers can extend the vessel's operational life and maintain safety standards even with added loads or altered design configurations.

Structural modifications, while beneficial for enhancing

functionality, introduce new fatigue risks that can compromise the safety and durability of marine vessels. By understanding the complex interactions between added loads, environmental stressors, and material properties, engineers can make informed decisions on reinforcement needs and fatigue management strategies. This ensures that structural modifications are safe and sustainable, maintaining the vessel's performance and longevity under diverse operational conditions.

2.3 Simulation in Structural Analysis

Keywords: Simulation, structural analysis, load assessment

Simulation has become an indispensable tool in structural analysis, providing engineers with accurate, cost-effective methods to predict and analyze the behavior of marine structures under various load conditions. In the context of maritime engineering, simulation enables the assessment of load impacts, stress distributions, and potential failure points without requiring extensive physical testing. This not only conserves resources but also enhances the precision of structural assessments, especially for complex vessels like catamarans with unique load-bearing characteristics (Lekatompessy & Zubaydi, 2019).

Role of Simulation in Load Assessment

One of the primary advantages of simulation in structural analysis is its capacity to model load assessments under real-world operational scenarios. Simulation software can replicate the effects of different load levels, revealing how stresses distribute across critical points in the structure, such as the hull and engine room. For aluminum alloy-based vessels, simulation is particularly valuable because it enables engineers to examine the material's response under diverse load intensities, identifying safe load thresholds and areas prone to fatigue. By utilizing these simulations, engineers can establish accurate load safety limits, ensuring the vessel's structural integrity and operational safety (Lekatompessy & Zubaydi, 2019).

Structural Analysis Using Simulation Techniques

Simulation in structural analysis typically involves several techniques, such as finite element analysis (FEA), which divides the structure into smaller, manageable sections called elements. By applying physical laws to each element, FEA allows engineers to analyze stress and strain distributions with high precision. This approach is especially beneficial for complex structures with intricate designs, as it provides a granular view of stress points and potential areas of structural weakness. For instance, in catamaran modifications, FEA can reveal how additional passenger loads above the engine room affect stress distributions, guiding engineers in making necessary reinforcements (Lekatompessy & Zubaydi, 2019).

Another critical application of simulation in structural analysis is in evaluating dynamic loads, such as those from wave impacts and engine vibrations. These cyclic loads can lead to fatigue over time, particularly in lightweight aluminum structures, which have specific stress tolerance levels. Simulation tools can predict how the structure will respond to these dynamic forces, allowing engineers to design reinforcements that mitigate fatigue risks and extend the vessel's operational life.

Cost-Effectiveness and Efficiency of Simulation

Traditional structural analysis methods, which rely on physical testing and full-scale prototypes, are often cost-prohibitive and time-consuming. Simulation addresses these limitations by offering a faster, more efficient way to perform structural assessments. Once a digital model of the structure is created, simulations can run various load scenarios and produce results that would be challenging and costly to replicate physically. This efficiency makes simulation a preferred approach in marine engineering, particularly in cases where structural modifications need frequent testing or adjustment (Lekatompessy &

Zubaydi, 2019).

Applications in Maritime Engineering and Future Directions

In maritime engineering, simulation has numerous applications, from initial design validation to post-modification assessments. By simulating the effects of structural changes before implementation, engineers can identify and mitigate potential issues, ensuring that the modifications will meet safety and performance standards. This process is especially valuable for high-speed vessels and catamarans, where even minor structural changes can significantly impact performance and safety.

As simulation technology advances, its applications in maritime engineering will continue to grow. The integration of machine learning with simulation models is an emerging trend, allowing simulations to predict structural behaviors with even greater accuracy based on historical data and real-time inputs. These developments promise to make simulation an even more powerful tool for structural analysis, enabling engineers to optimize vessel designs and modifications with minimal risk and cost.

Simulation has proven to be a highly effective tool in structural analysis, providing valuable insights into load assessments, stress distributions, and structural integrity without the need for costly physical tests. In marine applications, simulation enhances safety, efficiency, and precision, helping engineers to design and modify vessels with confidence. Through advanced simulation techniques, maritime engineering can ensure that structural modifications meet the required safety standards while minimizing resource expenditure.

III ANALYSIS AND SIMULATION METHODOLOGY

This chapter details the specific methods used to evaluate the structural integrity and load tolerance of aluminum alloy catamarans, particularly in the engine room deck area. The methodology includes a precise description of material properties, simulation parameters, and analytical techniques applied in static structural analysis and load simulation. Each aspect of the methodology is tailored to examine stress distribution patterns and to identify safe load thresholds, ensuring that the research findings are directly applicable to real-world maritime engineering scenarios. This structured approach allows for a focused assessment of load impacts, reinforcing areas of concern, and optimizing design recommendations based on simulation results.

3.1 Material and Mechanical Properties of Aluminum Alloy
Keywords: Young's Modulus, tensile strength, isotropic material

Aluminum alloy is widely chosen in marine applications due to its favorable mechanical properties, including high strength-to-weight ratio, corrosion resistance, and ease of fabrication. These properties make aluminum alloys suitable for high-speed vessels and catamarans, where weight reduction and structural durability are crucial. To effectively utilize aluminum in marine engineering, it is essential to understand its material and mechanical properties, including Young's Modulus, tensile strength, and its behavior as an isotropic material (Lekatompessy, 2021).

Young's Modulus and Structural Stiffness
Young's Modulus, also known as the modulus of elasticity, is a measure of a material's stiffness and resistance to elastic deformation under stress. For aluminum alloys commonly used in marine structures, Young's Modulus is approximately 71,000 MPa. This high modulus enables aluminum structures to withstand significant loads without permanent deformation, which is essential

for the dynamic environment of marine vessels, where they must endure varying forces due to wave impacts, engine vibrations, and other operational loads. A high Young's Modulus in aluminum alloy supports structural integrity and reduces deflection under load, enhancing the vessel's performance and stability in challenging marine conditions (Lekatompessy, 2021).

Tensile Strength and Load-Bearing Capacity

Tensile strength represents the maximum stress that a material can endure while being stretched or pulled before it breaks. Aluminum alloys used in marine structures typically offer tensile strengths in the range of 280-310 MPa, which is sufficient for handling the load requirements of high-speed vessels without excessive material bulk. This high tensile strength contributes to the ability of aluminum to bear operational loads efficiently while maintaining a lightweight structure. However, due to aluminum's moderate fatigue limit compared to other materials like steel, engineers must carefully consider load assessments to prevent fatigue over extended periods, especially in areas subject to cyclic loading, such as the hull and engine room decks (Lekatompessy, 2021).

Isotropic Properties of Aluminum Alloy

Aluminum alloy is considered an isotropic material, meaning it has uniform mechanical properties in all directions. This isotropic nature allows for consistent performance in various loading conditions, making it predictable and reliable for structural design. In marine engineering, the isotropic behavior of aluminum is advantageous because it ensures that stress distribution remains uniform across the structure, reducing the risk of unexpected weaknesses or failure points. This predictability supports robust design, enabling engineers to optimize load-bearing elements without needing excessive safety factors or additional reinforcement.

Implications for Marine Engineering Design

Understanding the mechanical properties of aluminum alloys

allows marine engineers to leverage its advantages in vessel design effectively. High Young's Modulus and tensile strength make aluminum alloys suitable for high-performance vessels where strength and weight efficiency are key. At the same time, aluminum's isotropic nature provides reliability in stress distribution, simplifying the structural analysis and reducing the need for complex reinforcement strategies. However, engineers must be mindful of aluminum's fatigue characteristics and design structural elements that avoid excessive cyclic loading to maximize the material's lifespan and maintain vessel safety.

The mechanical properties of aluminum alloy—high Young's Modulus, significant tensile strength, and isotropic behavior—make it a valuable material in marine applications, particularly for high-speed and lightweight vessels like catamarans. These properties support efficient, durable designs that meet the rigorous demands of maritime operations. Through a thorough understanding of these characteristics, engineers can develop optimized structures that balance strength, weight, and resilience, ensuring safe and effective marine engineering solutions.

3.2 Structural Simulation Procedures

Keywords: Static structural analysis, load simulation, maritime structures

Simulation is a fundamental component of structural analysis in maritime engineering, enabling precise assessments of how structures respond under different loading conditions. In the context of aluminum alloy catamarans, structural simulations allow engineers to evaluate load distributions, identify potential failure points, and determine the maximum safe load that the structure can sustain without compromising integrity. One of the most common and effective approaches is static structural analysis, which helps in understanding the effects of both fixed and variable loads in maritime environments. Through these simulation procedures, engineers gain valuable insights into the behavior of the vessel's structural elements, informing necessary reinforcements and modifications (Imron, 2014).

Static Structural Analysis in Maritime Engineering

Static structural analysis is a method that evaluates how a structure responds to loads that are applied slowly and remain constant over time. In the case of maritime structures, static analysis is used to assess stresses resulting from the weight of additional components, such as added passenger or cargo spaces, without considering time-varying or dynamic factors like waves or engine vibrations. For aluminum alloy structures, which can be sensitive to load concentrations, static structural analysis provides a baseline understanding of how the material will react under steady-state conditions, helping engineers determine safe load limits and potential stress points (Imron, 2014).

In catamaran applications, static structural analysis can be applied to simulate various loading scenarios on critical components like the engine room deck. This type of analysis helps in understanding whether the structure can handle added loads without exceeding the material's allowable stress. In cases where the load approaches or exceeds the structural limit, the analysis highlights areas that require reinforcement, guiding the design of modifications that enhance structural safety and durability.

Load Simulation Techniques

Load simulation is a specific procedure within static structural analysis that applies incremental loads to the digital model of the vessel, revealing stress distributions and deformation patterns across the structure. For example, by simulating loads from 0 to 5000 kN, engineers can observe how stress increases across the engine room deck of an aluminum alloy catamaran, identifying the maximum load that the structure can withstand within safe limits. Such incremental load simulations are critical in maritime engineering, where lightweight materials like aluminum must be carefully monitored for fatigue and deformation risks due to their relatively lower fatigue tolerance compared to other materials (Imron, 2014).

This step-by-step loading approach allows engineers to plot stress versus load graphs, which are then used to identify the exact point where stress reaches the material's allowable limit. These simulations also offer insights into the structure's behavior as load increases, including any potential points of deformation or failure. By examining these incremental responses, engineers can make data-driven decisions about reinforcing specific areas or limiting load to prevent fatigue or other structural failures.

Application of Simulation Results in Structural Design

The results obtained from structural simulation play a crucial role in the structural design and modification of maritime vessels. In particular, the findings from static structural analysis help engineers understand the exact load capacities of different sections of the vessel, such as the deck above the engine room. For aluminum alloy catamarans, simulation results reveal the need for additional structural stiffness if loads exceed a certain threshold, which can be achieved by increasing the cross-sectional area or modifying support structures.

For instance, if the static structural analysis shows that stress levels approach the aluminum alloy's yield strength at a load of 3000 kN, the simulation results would indicate that additional reinforcement is required if operational loads are expected to exceed this level. This approach enables engineers to optimize structural components, balancing weight and strength to achieve safe, efficient vessel designs. By using simulation-based insights, engineers can implement design improvements that enhance the structure's resilience and operational lifespan without resorting to extensive physical testing (Imron, 2014).

IV FINDINGS AND ANALYSIS

This chapter presents the findings from the simulations and analytical methods applied to assess the structural performance of the aluminum alloy catamaran, with a particular focus on the engine room deck. It provides a detailed analysis of stress distribution, load tolerance, and the effectiveness of structural reinforcements under varying load conditions. Graphs, tables, and visualizations illustrate the relationship between applied loads and resulting stresses, helping to identify the safety thresholds and potential failure points. The analysis in this chapter is integral to understanding the implications of load limits and guiding recommendations for optimal design and safety enhancements in maritime engineering.

4.1 Stress Distribution and Load Tolerance

Keywords: Stress distribution, load tolerance, structural failure

In the structural analysis of maritime vessels, understanding stress distribution and load tolerance is crucial for ensuring that all components can withstand operational loads without experiencing structural failure. Stress distribution refers to how stresses are spread across different areas of a structure when subjected to external forces, while load tolerance denotes the maximum load the structure can bear safely. For aluminum alloy catamarans, where lightweight design is essential, careful assessment of these factors is particularly critical, as exceeding load tolerance can lead to rapid structural degradation or failure. Through advanced simulation techniques, engineers can evaluate stress distribution patterns and establish safe load thresholds to optimize structural durability and performance (Tamimi, Soliman, & Khandel, 2023).

Stress Distribution in Maritime Structures

Stress distribution is influenced by the material properties, structural geometry, and load application points. In an aluminum alloy catamaran, which typically uses a lightweight structure, stress tends to concentrate in high-load regions, such as the engine room deck or hull sections directly impacted by wave forces. These stress concentrations are areas where the risk of fatigue cracks or other failures is elevated, especially in aluminum, which has lower fatigue resistance than some heavier metals. Identifying thcsc high-stress areas through simulation helps engineers make targeted design modifications, such as reinforcing specific points or redistributing loads, to prevent localized stress build-up and improve overall load tolerance (Tamimi et al., 2023).

For instance, a structural simulation may show that stress concentrates around joints or sharp corners, which are natural weak points in the structure. By analyzing these patterns, engineers can predict which areas are most vulnerable to fatigue and plan reinforcements accordingly. This approach helps maintain the vessel's structural integrity over time, even in high-stress environments, ensuring that critical areas do not exceed the material's load tolerance.

Determining Load Tolerance for Aluminum Structures

Load tolerance is the limit beyond which a structure cannot bear additional loads without risking damage or failure. For aluminum alloys, the load tolerance must be carefully determined to prevent deformation or fracture under operational loads. In marine vessels, factors such as wave impact, cargo weight, and passenger load contribute to the overall load demands, making load tolerance assessment essential to safe and efficient vessel design. Through static structural analysis and load simulation, engineers can gradually apply incremental loads to a digital model of the structure, observing how stress distributions change and identifying the maximum safe load before the stress reaches the material's yield strength (Tamimi et al., 2023).

In the case of a modified catamaran, this assessment may reveal that the engine room deck can withstand a load of up to 3000 kN without exceeding the aluminum alloy's allowable stress limit. If the load were to increase beyond this threshold, stress concentrations would reach a point where fatigue cracks or material failures could develop. Understanding this tolerance allows engineers to set operational limits, ensuring that the structure remains within safe stress levels even during peak loads.

Avoiding Structural Failure Through Load Management

Structural failure occurs when the load applied to a structure surpasses its load tolerance, leading to permanent deformation, cracking, or complete collapse. In the marine environment, structural failure can have severe consequences, potentially compromising vessel safety and endangering lives. To prevent this, load tolerance assessments enable engineers to determine the maximum load the structure can bear safely, guiding both design improvements and operational guidelines. For instance, if a simulation shows that load tolerance is reached at a particular load level, engineers can consider design modifications, such as increasing the cross-sectional area or using thicker material in high-stress zones, to prevent structural failure (Tamimi et al., 2023).

These simulation-based insights are especially valuable for aluminum alloy structures, where precise load management is required to prevent fatigue-related failures. By proactively reinforcing areas with high-stress concentrations or adjusting load-bearing components, engineers can extend the vessel's operational life and ensure safety standards are met.

Understanding stress distribution and load tolerance is key to preventing structural failure in aluminum alloy catamarans. Through simulation-based assessments, engineers can identify high-stress areas and establish safe load limits, ensuring that the structure remains robust under operational loads. By determining the maximum load tolerance and reinforcing critical areas, maritime engineers can enhance vessel safety and longevity, providing a reliable framework for managing load-related risks in lightweight marine structures.

4.2 Safe Load Limits for Catamaran Engine Room
Keywords: Safe load, engine room, aluminum alloy

Determining safe load limits is essential for maintaining the structural integrity of critical areas in catamarans, such as the engine room. The engine room deck of a catamaran, typically constructed from aluminum alloy to reduce weight and improve fuel efficiency, must be carefully assessed to handle added loads without exceeding the allowable stress thresholds of the material. Establishing these safe load limits ensures that the aluminum alloy structure can support operational demands safely, minimizing the risk of structural fatigue or failure over time.

Defining Safe Load Limits in Aluminum Alloy Structures

Safe load limits refer to the maximum load a structure can support without experiencing excessive stress or deformation that could lead to material failure. For aluminum alloy structures, these limits are particularly critical due to the material's relatively lower fatigue resistance compared to heavier metals. In the engine room, where machinery and potentially additional cargo or passenger areas are located, loads can vary significantly, creating high-stress regions that, if not properly managed, could accelerate fatigue and lead to structural compromise.

Using load simulations and static structural analysis, engineers can apply incremental loads to the digital model of the engine room deck to determine the exact load level at which the aluminum alloy approaches its allowable stress limit. For instance, simulations may reveal that the engine room deck can safely support up to 3000 kN without exceeding the material's yield strength. This threshold acts as a guideline for safe operation, helping to ensure that added loads—whether from machinery, equipment, or modifications like passenger compartments—remain within limits that the structure can tolerate without undergoing permanent deformation or cracking.

Simulation-Based Determination of Load Limits

Simulations are integral to establishing safe load limits because they enable detailed analysis of how stress distributes across the engine room deck under varying loads. By observing stress patterns and points of concentration, engineers can determine the maximum load that maintains safety without approaching the failure threshold. In catamarans, this process is especially important due to the lightweight design and high-speed operation, which place unique demands on the aluminum alloy structure. Simulations help quantify these demands, offering engineers a clear understanding of the deck's load-bearing capacity and the areas that might require reinforcement for added safety.

For example, if simulation results indicate that stress levels approach the material's limit when the load reaches around 3000 kN, this value would be set as the safe load limit. Any operation or modification that might increase the load beyond this point would require either structural reinforcements or design adjustments to maintain safety standards. This proactive approach prevents overloading and contributes to the long-term durability of the vessel, as it minimizes the risk of fatigue-induced cracking or failure in the engine room deck.

Reinforcement Strategies for Exceeding Safe Load Limits

In cases where operational needs or modifications demand loads beyond the established safe limit, reinforcement strategies must be employed to strengthen the structure. For aluminum alloy decks, increasing the cross-sectional area or adding support elements can help redistribute the load and enhance the structure's ability to handle additional stress without exceeding safe levels. Such reinforcements might involve thickening the deck plate or adding support beams to high-stress areas, thereby raising the deck's load tolerance and accommodating new load requirements without risking structural compromise.

These reinforcement strategies, informed by simulation data, ensure that the engine room deck can safely support higher loads if needed, aligning with both safety standards and functional requirements. By setting safe load limits and reinforcing the structure as necessary, engineers maintain the vessel's performance capabilities while safeguarding against the risks associated with excessive stress on aluminum alloy components.

Safe load limits are a foundational aspect of structural design and safety in catamarans, particularly in critical areas like the engine room deck constructed from aluminum alloy. Through simulation-based load analysis, engineers can define these limits precisely, ensuring that the structure remains within safe operational boundaries. When load demands exceed the established limits, targeted reinforcement measures provide additional strength, extending the deck's load tolerance and preserving the vessel's structural integrity under increased load conditions.

4.3 Visualization of Safety Thresholds

Keywords: Stress vs. load graph, safety threshold, structural integrity

Visualizing safety thresholds is crucial for understanding and communicating the structural limits of catamaran components, particularly the engine room deck, which is subject to varying loads. A primary tool for this is the stress vs. load graph, which graphically represents the relationship between applied loads and the resulting stress on the structure. By plotting load increments against the stress they induce, engineers can identify the exact point, or threshold, where stress levels approach the material's allowable limit. This visualization aids in assessing structural integrity, as it provides a clear and immediate understanding of how close the structure is to failure under specific loads, guiding decisions for safe operation and necessary reinforcements.

Stress vs. Load Graphs and Safety Thresholds

A stress vs. load graph is typically created by incrementally applying loads to a digital model of the structure through simulation, allowing engineers to observe the resulting stress levels at each load point. In this graph, the x-axis represents the applied load, while the y-axis indicates the corresponding stress levels within the structure. As load increases, stress also rises, following a trend until it approaches a critical threshold, often marked as the yield strength or maximum allowable stress of the material. For aluminum alloy used in catamarans, this threshold is essential in defining the safe load limits, as any load that generates stress beyond this limit risks structural compromise or failure (Tamimi, Soliman, & Khandel, 2023).

In the context of an aluminum alloy engine room deck, such a graph allows engineers to visualize at what load level the stress approaches the alloy's safe operating limit, which might be around 300 MPa. The point where the stress curve intersects this allowable stress line represents the maximum load that the structure can handle safely. This visual tool, therefore, provides a clear benchmark, ensuring that operational loads stay within safe boundaries and highlighting when reinforcements are necessary for loads beyond the threshold.

Importance of Visualizing Safety Thresholds

Visualizing safety thresholds using stress vs. load graphs is crucial in structural analysis for several reasons:

1. Preventing Overloading: It helps engineers determine safe operational limits by showing where stress levels start to reach critical values, preventing accidental overloading that could lead to structural fatigue or failure.
2. Guiding Structural Reinforcements: When loads exceed safety thresholds, the graph highlights the need for reinforcements, allowing engineers to proactively strengthen specific areas and ensure that even increased loads remain within safe limits.
3. Ensuring Structural Integrity: By monitoring how stress varies with load, engineers can make informed decisions to maintain structural integrity, reducing the risk of fatigue-related issues

and extending the structure's lifespan under operational conditions (Tamimi et al., 2023).

Applications in Catamaran Design and Operation

In the design and operational phases of catamarans, stress vs. load graphs provide a visual reference that aids both engineers and operators in understanding the vessel's load tolerance. During design, these graphs help in choosing materials and structural modifications that ensure durability and safety. For operators, the visualization can serve as a guideline for maintaining load within safe limits during actual use, such as avoiding additional loads that might push the structure beyond the allowable stress threshold.

For example, if a catamaran's engine room deck is shown to tolerate up to 3000 kN without exceeding the safe stress threshold, operators can monitor loads to avoid surpassing this limit. If operational needs demand higher loads, engineers can use the graph to assess where additional support is required, such as adding reinforcements to increase the load-bearing capacity without risking structural integrity.

Stress vs. load graphs are valuable visual tools for defining and communicating safety thresholds in catamaran structures. By clearly displaying how stress levels correspond to load increments, these graphs help prevent overloading, guide necessary reinforcements, and maintain structural integrity. In aluminum alloy catamarans, where weight and durability must be balanced, this visualization ensures that all structural modifications and load applications remain within safe and efficient operating limits.

V IMPLICATIONS OF FINDINGS ON STRUCTURAL DESIGN AND SAFETY

This chapter delves into the implications of the findings for structural design, load management, and safety enhancements in aluminum alloy catamarans. It interprets key results—such as identified safety thresholds, stress distribution, and reinforcement effectiveness—and examines how these insights can be applied to strengthen high-stress areas, particularly around the engine room deck. The discussion connects these findings with practical applications, highlighting how adherence to defined load limits and strategic reinforcements can improve structural integrity, enhance vessel lifespan, and ensure operational safety. By linking analytical outcomes to design and safety practices, this chapter provides a framework for implementing effective load management and reinforcement strategies in future maritime engineering projects.

5.1 Implications of Load Limits on Structural Design
Keywords: Structural design, load implications, maritime engineering

Establishing load limits is a critical factor in the structural design of marine vessels, particularly for lightweight aluminum alloy catamarans. The implications of these load limits extend beyond safety, influencing fundamental aspects of the vessel's design, material selection, and structural reinforcements. In maritime engineering, understanding and applying load limits ensures that vessels can perform under operational demands while minimizing the risk of structural fatigue and failure. By incorporating well-defined load limits into the design phase, engineers can optimize vessel performance, extend service life, and maintain compliance with safety standards.

Influence of Load Limits on Material and Structural Choices

The need to adhere to safe load limits directly impacts the materials chosen for various components. For instance, aluminum alloy, while lightweight and corrosion-resistant, has specific load-bearing capabilities and a lower fatigue threshold compared to other marine materials like steel. As a result, designers must ensure that structural elements, such as the engine room deck, are capable of supporting intended loads without exceeding the alloy's safe stress limit. This often involves evaluating the maximum operational loads and choosing a material grade that can balance weight efficiency with the required strength, taking into account potential load variations due to environmental factors such as wave impact and vessel motion (Tamimi, Soliman, & Khandel, 2023).

When load limits are precisely defined, engineers can make targeted design decisions, such as adjusting the thickness of the deck or reinforcing high-stress areas. This ensures that the structure remains within safe operational thresholds, reducing the likelihood of overloading that could compromise the aluminum alloy's integrity. Furthermore, defining load limits in the early design stages supports efficient material use, avoiding unnecessary weight additions that could reduce speed and fuel efficiency.

Designing for Load Distribution and Structural Integrity

One of the primary challenges in marine structural design is achieving an even load distribution across critical components. Load limits guide engineers in designing structural layouts that prevent excessive stress concentrations, particularly in areas like the engine room, which supports substantial machinery and may accommodate additional loads from modifications. By setting clear load limits, engineers can design the structure to handle distributed loads effectively, reducing localized stress and enhancing the vessel's overall stability and durability (Tamimi et al., 2023).

For instance, the use of load limits may lead to design adjustments, such as integrating additional support beams or cross-sectional reinforcements in the deck structure. These adjustments distribute loads more evenly, ensuring that no single area bears excessive stress. Such design considerations are particularly important in aluminum alloy catamarans, where improper load distribution can accelerate fatigue and reduce structural lifespan. Additionally, load limits provide guidelines for incorporating structural flexibility, enabling the vessel to absorb and adapt to dynamic maritime forces without compromising integrity.

Implications for Safety and Regulatory Compliance

In maritime engineering, adhering to established load limits is essential for compliance with safety regulations and standards. Regulatory bodies mandate specific structural requirements to ensure vessel safety, and failing to meet these standards can lead to operational restrictions or even legal liabilities. By incorporating load limits into the structural design process, marine engineers can ensure that vessels meet both national and international safety requirements, preventing potential operational interruptions or costly retrofitting needs in the future.

In addition to regulatory compliance, defined load limits support onboard safety by reducing the risk of structural failure during operations. This is particularly vital for high-speed vessels like catamarans, which experience varied stress levels due to wave impacts, high speeds, and frequent loading and unloading cycles. Setting and adhering to safe load limits not only protects the structure but also enhances crew and passenger safety, providing a reliable framework for safe maritime operations (Tamimi et al., 2023).

Optimizing Design for Performance and Longevity

Load limits are also instrumental in balancing performance with durability. By understanding and applying these limits in the design phase, engineers can create vessels that perform optimally under operational loads while maintaining structural resilience over time. For instance, in a catamaran, where speed and fuel efficiency are crucial, adhering to load limits prevents overloading that could hinder performance, ensuring that the vessel remains lightweight and agile. At the same time, safe load limits minimize the risk of fatigue-related issues, extending the structural lifespan and reducing maintenance costs associated with material degradation.

Designing with load limits in mind ultimately results in a more resilient and efficient vessel. Through carefully managed load applications and structural reinforcements, catamarans can achieve the desired balance of safety, durability, and operational efficiency, contributing to sustainable maritime engineering practices.

Load limits play a fundamental role in the structural design of aluminum alloy catamarans, influencing material selection, load distribution, safety compliance, and performance optimization. By defining and integrating these limits early in the design process, engineers can create structures that meet operational demands while maintaining structural integrity and safety standards. In maritime engineering, such design principles contribute to more reliable and efficient vessel designs, supporting long-term sustainability and safety in marine operations.

5.2 Enhancing Structural Stiffness for Load Management

Keywords: Structural stiffness, modulus of cross-section, load management

Structural stiffness is a critical factor in managing loads effectively in marine vessels, especially those constructed with lightweight materials like aluminum alloy. In catamarans, enhancing structural stiffness is essential to ensure the vessel can withstand operational loads without experiencing excessive deformation or compromising safety.

By increasing stiffness, typically through adjustments in the modulus of the cross-section, engineers can enhance the structure's resistance to bending and stress concentrations, thus improving load management and extending the vessel's durability under varying loads.

Role of Structural Stiffness in Load Management

Structural stiffness refers to a material's resistance to deformation when a force is applied. In maritime engineering, increased stiffness allows the structure to maintain its shape and integrity under loads, thereby ensuring that stress is effectively distributed and that localized deformations are minimized. For aluminum alloy catamarans, which are designed to be lightweight yet robust, maintaining appropriate stiffness is critical for load management, particularly in high-stress areas like the engine room deck, where loads from machinery and potential passenger additions are concentrated. Without sufficient stiffness, these areas are at risk of excessive deflection, leading to fatigue and potential structural failure.

By enhancing stiffness, engineers can create a structure that is better able to manage operational loads, effectively transferring stress across the vessel without risking localized deformation or material fatigue. This improved load distribution is essential for aluminum structures, as the material's relatively lower fatigue resistance makes it sensitive to stress concentrations that can lead to cracking over time.

Modulus of Cross-Section as a Factor in Stiffness Enhancement

The modulus of the cross-section, often referred to as the section modulus, is a geometric property that measures the ability of a cross-sectional shape to resist bending. Increasing the modulus of the cross-section enhances structural stiffness, making the structure more capable of withstanding applied loads without excessive bending. For aluminum alloy structures, adjustments to the cross-section, such as thickening critical load-bearing sections or altering the shape to distribute stress more evenly, can significantly increase stiffness and improve load management.

In the case of a catamaran's engine room deck, where added passenger or cargo loads can increase stress on the deck, increasing the section modulus might involve thickening the deck plate or adding supportive beams beneath high-stress areas. These adjustments distribute the load more evenly across the deck, ensuring that the structure remains within safe stress limits even when subjected to high operational loads. By optimizing the cross-sectional modulus, engineers enhance the vessel's stiffness, allowing it to bear additional loads with minimal deformation, thereby reducing the risk of fatigue-related failures.

Structural Reinforcements and Load Management Strategies

Structural stiffness can also be enhanced through reinforcements that strengthen load-bearing sections and prevent localized deformation under concentrated loads. For aluminum alloy catamarans, reinforcements may include the addition of ribs, frames, or girders in areas where stiffness needs to be maximized. These reinforcements work in tandem with adjustments to the cross-sectional modulus, increasing the structure's ability to manage loads effectively without compromising weight efficiency.

For example, if simulation and analysis show that the engine room deck reaches critical stress levels under high loads, adding reinforced beams or ribs beneath the deck can help dissipate stress across a broader area, preventing specific points from bearing excessive load. This strategy not only increases stiffness but also improves the vessel's resilience to cyclical loading, reducing fatigue accumulation over time. Additionally, by carefully positioning these reinforcements, engineers can achieve optimal stiffness without adding unnecessary weight, which is essential for maintaining the vessel's speed and fuel efficiency.

Benefits of Enhanced Stiffness in Aluminum Alloy Vessels

Enhanced structural stiffness provides several benefits in managing loads and maintaining the structural integrity of aluminum alloy catamarans:

1. Improved Load Distribution: By increasing stiffness, stress is

more evenly distributed across the structure, reducing the risk of localized deformation and material fatigue.

2. Increased Load Tolerance: A stiffer structure can handle higher loads without reaching critical stress thresholds, enabling the vessel to carry additional weight safely.

3. Extended Structural Lifespan: Enhanced stiffness reduces deformation and fatigue risks, prolonging the life of the vessel and decreasing maintenance costs associated with fatigue-related damage.

4. Maintained Operational Efficiency: Stiffness enhancements allow the vessel to manage loads more effectively without adding significant weight, preserving its performance, speed, and fuel efficiency.

Enhancing structural stiffness through adjustments to the modulus of the cross-section and targeted reinforcements is an effective strategy for load management in aluminum alloy catamarans. By improving stiffness, engineers can ensure that the vessel can safely handle operational loads, distribute stress effectively, and minimize the risks associated with material fatigue. This approach to structural design supports safe, efficient, and durable marine vessels that meet the performance demands of modern maritime engineering.

5.3 Recommendations for Future Research
Keywords: Deformation, dynamic load, structural simulation

While this study provides valuable insights into load management and structural integrity for aluminum alloy catamarans, there are several areas where further research could enhance understanding and improve design practices. Future research should focus on more complex factors such as deformation under dynamic loads and advanced structural simulation techniques, which could provide a deeper and more comprehensive understanding of how aluminum structures respond to real-world maritime conditions.

1. Deformation Analysis in Aluminum Alloy Structures

Future studies should delve deeper into the deformation characteristics of aluminum alloy structures, particularly under high-stress and cyclical loading conditions. While static load assessments are effective in defining baseline load limits, they do not fully capture the deformation behavior under dynamic loads, such as wave impacts, wind, and engine vibrations. Analyzing deformation in such scenarios would provide a clearer picture of long-term structural integrity, identifying areas that may be susceptible to gradual degradation. Advanced deformation analysis could also support the development of innovative reinforcement strategies that focus on areas with the highest risk of deformation and fatigue.

Research into time-dependent deformation or "creep" in aluminum alloy structures could further refine load management practices. Since aluminum has different creep characteristics than heavier materials like steel, understanding how it behaves over extended periods under constant stress will be valuable, especially for vessels with prolonged operation in harsh conditions. Future research could include experiments and simulations focused on aluminum's deformation properties over time, enhancing durability in high-stress marine applications.

2. Impact of Dynamic Loads on Structural Fatigue

Dynamic loads represent a complex aspect of structural analysis in marine vessels, as they involve fluctuating forces from waves, wind, and vessel movements. Future research should explore the effects of dynamic loading on aluminum alloy structures, as these loads induce cyclical stress that can lead to accelerated fatigue. Dynamic load simulation would provide insights into how these forces interact with the material's fatigue properties, particularly in high-speed vessels like catamarans that experience frequent and variable loading conditions.

Incorporating dynamic load effects into fatigue analysis could result in more robust design standards, optimizing the placement of reinforcements in areas that bear the brunt of fluctuating stresses. By simulating real-world maritime conditions, such research would allow engineers to predict where fatigue cracks are likely to initiate, improving preventive measures and extending the vessel's operational life. Research into the combined effects of wave-induced loads and operational vibrations could yield new insights into optimizing the aluminum structure for resilience under diverse and complex loading conditions.

3. Advances in Structural Simulation Techniques

As computational technology advances, structural simulation is becoming increasingly sophisticated, enabling engineers to model more realistic scenarios. Future research could benefit from exploring advanced simulation techniques that integrate finite element analysis (FEA) with real-time data inputs and machine learning. By leveraging these technologies, structural simulations could become more predictive, allowing for more accurate modeling of stress distributions and deformation patterns over time.

For instance, machine learning algorithms could be trained on existing data to predict structural weaknesses in new vessel designs based on historical performance. Such predictive simulations could identify potential failure points early in the design process, saving time and resources in physical testing. Additionally, multi-physics simulations that incorporate thermal, structural, and fluid dynamics aspects would provide a holistic view of how aluminum alloy structures respond to combined environmental factors, leading to more resilient and adaptable structural designs.

4. Experimental Validation of Simulation Models

While simulations provide significant theoretical insights, experimental validation is essential to confirm their accuracy. Future research should include experimental studies that replicate the load conditions modeled in simulations, particularly for dynamic loads. This experimental approach could validate simulation models, improving their reliability and making them more widely applicable across different vessel types and operational conditions. Experimental validation is particularly critical for understanding material behavior under multi-axial stresses, which are common in marine environments but challenging to replicate accurately in purely simulated models.

Experiments could include scale model testing in controlled environments or full-scale testing under monitored conditions, allowing researchers to observe material responses and validate the predicted structural behavior. By comparing experimental results with simulation outputs, engineers could refine simulation parameters and improve the accuracy of predictive models, ultimately leading to safer and more reliable vessel designs.

Research into aluminum alloy catamarans can benefit significantly from future studies focused on deformation under dynamic loading, advanced simulation techniques, and experimental validation. By exploring these areas, researchers can deepen understanding of the material's behavior under real-world maritime conditions, paving the way for enhanced structural resilience and load management strategies. Such advancements would contribute to the field of maritime engineering, supporting the development of safer, more efficient vessels capable of withstanding diverse environmental challenges.

VI CONCLUSIONS AND RECOMMENDATIONS

This final chapter summarizes the key insights and outcomes of the study, reinforcing the importance of defined safety limits, load management, and structural reinforcement in aluminum alloy catamarans. It consolidates the findings on stress distribution, load tolerance, and reinforcement effectiveness, highlighting their practical implications for safer and more resilient vessel design. Additionally, the chapter provides targeted recommendations for future design enhancements, operational guidelines, and areas for further research, aiming to support advancements in maritime safety and engineering practices. This conclusion offers a cohesive reflection on the study's contributions to naval engineering and outlines actionable steps for future applications in the field.

6.1 Summary of Findings

Keywords: Safety limits, structural reinforcement, maritime safety

This study has examined the critical factors involved in maintaining the structural integrity and operational safety of aluminum alloy catamarans, specifically focusing on load-bearing capabilities in the engine room deck. The findings underscore the importance of establishing precise safety limits and implementing structural reinforcements to manage the unique demands imposed on lightweight marine vessels. By defining these parameters, engineers can ensure that the structure remains robust under operational loads, contributing to enhanced maritime safety and prolonged vessel lifespan.

Key Findings on Safety Limits

The study establishes that safety limits for load-bearing components, particularly in the engine room deck, are crucial to prevent structural failure. Through simulation and load assessment, the research identifies the maximum safe load that the aluminum alloy structure can support without risking material fatigue or deformation. For instance, the engine room deck's safe load threshold was determined based on stress vs. load analysis, ensuring that operational loads do not exceed the material's allowable stress limits. Adhering to these safety limits prevents overloading and reduces the risk of structural failure, which is essential for maintaining the safety and reliability of high-speed catamarans (Tamimi, Soliman, & Khandel, 2023).

Importance of Structural Reinforcement

The findings also highlight the necessity of structural reinforcements in areas where load demands exceed the aluminum alloy's inherent capacity. When loads approach or surpass the established safety limits, structural reinforcements, such as increasing the modulus of the cross-section or adding support beams, are essential to distribute stress more evenly and enhance stiffness. These reinforcements ensure that the vessel can safely accommodate additional loads, such as passenger or cargo weight, without compromising structural integrity. The targeted reinforcement of high-stress areas not only bolsters the structure against fatigue but also extends the vessel's operational lifespan by mitigating the risks associated with cyclical loading and stress concentration.

Contribution to Maritime Safety

Overall, this study's findings contribute significantly to maritime safety by providing a framework for safe load limits and reinforcement strategies in aluminum alloy vessels. By setting clear safety thresholds and reinforcing critical areas, engineers can design vessels that perform reliably and safely under varying load conditions. These practices are vital in the context of lightweight catamarans, which prioritize speed and efficiency but require meticulous load management to maintain structural resilience. Implementing these safety-focused design strategies supports the broader goals of maritime safety, ensuring that vessels operate within safe limits and reducing the likelihood of structural failure due to overloading or fatigue.

The study establishes the critical role of safety limits and structural reinforcements in managing load-bearing demands in aluminum alloy catamarans. By adhering to these parameters, maritime engineers can enhance the vessel's durability, safety, and performance. These findings provide valuable guidance for the design and operational practices of lightweight marine vessels, aligning with maritime safety standards and contributing to safer, more resilient maritime operations.

6.2 Practical Applications

Keywords: Maritime design, catamaran modifications, safety engineering

The findings of this study have direct applications in the fields of maritime design, catamaran modifications, and safety engineering, providing valuable insights for engineers, designers, and operators in the marine industry. By integrating defined safety limits and structural reinforcements into practical applications, the industry can improve both the safety and performance of aluminum alloy catamarans, especially when modifications and load adjustments are necessary. These applications ensure that vessels operate efficiently within safe boundaries, promoting sustainable and resilient maritime practices.

Guiding Maritime Design with Safety Limits

The establishment of clear safety limits for aluminum alloy catamarans is foundational in guiding maritime design. Engineers can use these safety thresholds as a baseline to determine the appropriate material specifications and structural layouts that meet operational demands while ensuring long-term durability. By incorporating safety limits into the initial design phase, engineers can avoid overdesigning or underestimating structural requirements, achieving an optimal balance between weight, strength, and load tolerance. This approach is particularly beneficial for high-speed vessels where weight efficiency and structural integrity are both critical for performance and safety.

Additionally, safety limits aid in material selection and structural reinforcement decisions, allowing designers to choose the most suitable aluminum alloy grades and configure the vessel's layout to distribute loads evenly. These considerations enhance both the operational efficiency and structural resilience of the vessel, enabling it to withstand the dynamic loads encountered during high-speed and high-capacity operations (Tamimi, Soliman, & Khandel, 2023).

Supporting Catamaran Modifications with Reinforcement Strategies

The practical application of reinforcement strategies is essential for catamaran modifications, especially when new passenger areas, cargo spaces, or equipment are added. By using the study's findings on load limits and stress distribution, maritime engineers can implement targeted reinforcements in high-stress areas, such as the engine room deck. This ensures that modifications do not compromise structural integrity or exceed the established safety limits, allowing the vessel to accommodate additional loads safely.

For example, when passenger compartments are added above the engine room, reinforcement measures such as increasing the cross-sectional modulus or adding structural beams can distribute the additional load, reducing stress concentrations and maintaining stability. These reinforcement strategies allow catamarans to adapt to evolving operational needs, supporting flexible design modifications without compromising safety or structural integrity.

Enhancing Safety Engineering Practices in Marine Operations

The principles of safety engineering emphasized in this study can be applied to improve overall maritime safety practices, particularly in routine load management and maintenance. Operators can use the study's stress vs. load findings to set operational load guidelines, ensuring that loads remain within safe limits during voyages. This proactive approach to load management minimizes the risk of fatigue and structural failure, safeguarding both the vessel and its occupants.

In maintenance, safety engineering practices informed by this study can help identify high-stress areas that require regular inspections or reinforcements. For example, engineers can focus on areas near load concentration points, monitoring for early signs of fatigue or cracking and conducting preventative maintenance as necessary. This focus on safety-driven maintenance practices enhances vessel reliability and reduces the likelihood of unexpected repairs or downtimes due to structural issues.

Optimizing Maritime Operations for Performance and Longevity

Practical applications of load limits and reinforcements contribute to optimizing the overall performance and lifespan of aluminum alloy catamarans. By maintaining the vessel's structural integrity through adherence to safety limits and strategic reinforcements, operators can achieve better fuel efficiency, reduced maintenance costs, and extended operational life. This optimization supports both economic and environmental sustainability in maritime operations, as lightweight, high-speed vessels can perform at their best while minimizing resource consumption and maintenance needs.

Additionally, the study's findings support the industry's transition toward more resilient and adaptable vessel designs, enabling aluminum alloy catamarans to operate safely under varying load conditions and environmental factors. These optimized design practices align with modern maritime engineering goals, which prioritize both safety and efficiency in vessel operations.

The practical applications of this study's findings in maritime design, catamaran modifications, and safety engineering reinforce the importance of integrating safety limits and structural reinforcements into the design and operational phases. By applying these principles, the maritime industry can enhance vessel safety, accommodate modifications effectively, and improve the performance and longevity of aluminum alloy catamarans. These applications contribute to safer and more adaptable vessels, supporting the continued advancement of maritime engineering and sustainable marine operations.

6.3 Final Recommendations

Keywords: Load management, structural integrity, safety enhancement

The insights from this study underline the critical role of effective load management, structural integrity, and safety enhancement in the design and operation of aluminum alloy catamarans. These recommendations aim to guide maritime engineers, designers, and operators in applying safe design principles and load management strategies to maintain vessel integrity and improve safety. By focusing on these aspects, the industry can ensure that aluminum alloy catamarans operate within safe limits, meeting both performance and safety standards over their operational lifespan.

1. Prioritize Accurate Load Management

Accurate load management is essential to avoid overloading and prevent structural fatigue in aluminum alloy catamarans. It is recommended that designers and operators set precise load thresholds based on the vessel's stress vs. load analyses. These thresholds should guide both design decisions and operational practices, ensuring that added loads—such as passenger or cargo weight remain within safe boundaries.

Operationally, load management practices should include routine monitoring and adherence to the established load limits. Operators should avoid temporary or permanent loads that exceed these limits, as even slight overloading can lead to fatigue and compromise the vessel's structural integrity over time. Additionally, implementing load distribution techniques that evenly spread weight across the structure can further enhance stability and reduce the risk of concentrated stress points that could lead to structural failure

(Tamimi, Soliman, & Khandel, 2023).

2. Reinforce High-Stress Areas to Maintain Structural Integrity

In aluminum alloy catamarans, reinforcing high-stress areas is crucial for maintaining structural integrity, especially when load demands increase due to modifications or operational needs. It is recommended that engineers incorporate additional structural reinforcements in areas identified as prone to stress concentration, such as the engine room deck, where added passenger or equipment loads are often applied.

For effective reinforcement, adjustments to the modulus of the cross-section or the addition of support beams are advised. These measures help distribute stress evenly, prevent localized deformation, and ensure that the structure can accommodate higher loads safely. Engineers should consider reinforcing these areas during both the design phase and when modifications are made, ensuring that structural integrity is preserved across all load conditions.

3. Implement Regular Inspections and Preventive Maintenance for Safety Enhancement

To enhance safety, regular inspections and preventive maintenance are recommended for aluminum alloy catamarans, especially in high-stress areas prone to fatigue. Routine inspections should focus on identifying early signs of stress-related degradation, such as cracks or material fatigue, particularly around joints and load-bearing sections. Detecting these issues early allows for timely reinforcements or repairs, which can prevent structural failure and extend the vessel's lifespan.

In addition to inspections, preventive maintenance programs should include reinforcement of critical areas based on load history and operational data. Areas that experience cyclical loading, such as the hull and deck, may benefit from periodic reinforcement to address wear and tear from dynamic marine conditions. Such proactive safety measures ensure that aluminum alloy catamarans remain structurally sound and continue to meet safety standards under diverse operational scenarios (Tamimi et al., 2023).

4. Leverage Advanced Structural Simulations for Load and Stress Analysis

Advanced structural simulations should be utilized in both the design and modification stages to accurately predict how aluminum alloy catamarans will respond to various load conditions. By leveraging finite element analysis (FEA) and dynamic load simulations, engineers can model real-world conditions, observing how different load scenarios impact stress distribution and identifying any potential points of failure.

Incorporating simulation results into the design process enables engineers to make informed decisions on structural adjustments and reinforcements, ensuring that the vessel operates within safe stress limits. Simulation-based design also provides a foundation for developing safety guidelines that are tailored to specific load requirements, supporting the creation of safer and more resilient vessel structures.

5. Educate Operators and Crew on Safe Load Management Practices

A critical aspect of safety enhancement is ensuring that vessel operators and crew understand and follow safe load management practices. It is recommended that maritime organizations provide training for crew members on load distribution, operational load limits, and the importance of adhering to these safety guidelines. Educating operators about load management reduces the risk of unintentional overloading and ensures that crew members make informed decisions about cargo and passenger placement on board.

Additionally, safety protocols should be established and regularly reinforced, emphasizing the importance of following load limits and conducting routine checks to ensure compliance. By creating a safety-conscious operational culture, maritime organizations can enhance both the safety and longevity of aluminum alloy catamarans.

These final recommendations provide a roadmap for improving the load management, structural integrity, and safety of aluminum alloy catamarans. By prioritizing load accuracy, reinforcing high-stress areas, conducting regular maintenance, leveraging simulations, and educating crew, the maritime industry can achieve safer, more efficient vessel operations. Implementing these strategies ensures that aluminum alloy catamarans maintain structural integrity and meet safety standards, contributing to a more resilient and reliable maritime fleet.

REFERENCES

Cheng, X., Feng, B., Liu, Z., & Chang, H. (2018). Hull surface modification for ship resistance performance optimization based on Delaunay triangulation. *Ocean Engineering*, 153, 333–344. https://doi.org/10.1016/j.oceaneng.2018.01.109

Feng, L., Li, D., Shi, H., Zhang, Q., & Wang, S. (2020). A study on the ultimate strength of ship plate with coupled corrosion and crack damage. *Ocean Engineering*, 200, 106950. https://doi.org/10.1016/j.oceaneng.2020.106950

Hosseinabadi, O. F., & Khedmati, M. R. (2021). A review on ultimate strength of aluminium structural elements and systems for marine applications. *Ocean Engineering*, 232, 109153. https://doi.org/10.1016/j.oceaneng.2021.109153

Imron, A. (2014). Kerusakan struktur akibat getaran lokal pada kapal yang jarang diperhatikan; Analisis dan solusi (Studi kasus). *Jurnal Kelautan Nasional*, 9(1), 11–19. https://doi.org/10.15578/jkn.v9i1.6198

Lekatompessy, D. R. (2021). The effect analysis of the stiffness changes of a Traditional Fishing Boat Foundation on Vibration Amplitude. *TEKNIK*, 42(1), 71–78. https://doi.org/10.14710/TEKNIK.V42I1.30978

Lekatompessy, D. R., & Zubaydi, A. (2019). The effect of joints model to the vibration characteristics of wood. *IOP Conference Series: Earth and Environmental Science*, 339(1), 012038. https://doi.org/10.1088/1755-1315/339/1/012038

Magoga, T., Aksu, S., & Slater, K. (2023). Implementation of a nominal stress approach for the fatigue assessment of aluminium naval ships. *Procedia Structural Integrity*, 45, 28–35. https://doi.org/10.1016/j.prostr.2023.05.010

Tamimi, M. F., Soliman, M., & Khandel, O. (2023). Quantifying reliability of ship hulls under propagating fatigue cracks. *Ocean Engineering*, 279, 114488. https://doi.org/10.1016/j.oceaneng.2023.114488

Takeuchi, T., Osawa, N., Tatsumi, A., Inoue, T., Hirakawa, S., Seki, N., Yoshida, T., Miratsu, R., & Ikeda, S. (2023). Fatigue assessment of ship structures based on equivalent wave probability (EWP) concept (1st report): Proposal of EWP concept and its verification by 8600TEU container ship's onboard hull monitoring. *Marine Structures*, 91, 103476. https://doi.org/10.1016/j.marstruc.2023.103476

ABOUT THE AUTHOR

Dr. Debby R. Lekatompessy is an accomplished expert in naval engineering, associated with the Department of Naval Engineering at the Faculty of Engineering, Pattimura University. Her extensive practical experience and contributions have had a substantial impact on advancing knowledge and practices within the maritime field.

Her academic path began at Pattimura University, where she completed her bachelor's degree in Naval Engineering. Driven by a commitment to deeper expertise, she pursued and attained a master's degree in the same field. Throughout her studies, she demonstrated a strong academic aptitude and a keen interest in the development of maritime technology and systems.

As a dedicated researcher and educator, Dr. Debby R. Lekatompessy has been involved in numerous research projects focused on naval engineering. Her research interests encompass ship design, maritime sustainability, propulsion systems, and the management of maritime energy. She has published multiple scholarly articles that contribute significantly to the understanding and advancement of maritime technology.

In addition to her research, Dr. Debby actively participates in teaching and mentoring at Pattimura University, sharing her knowledge and practical insights with students. Her role as an educator is pivotal in inspiring future engineers, encouraging them to explore the opportunities in naval engineering, and instilling a comprehensive understanding of the field.

Dr. Debby R. Lekatompessy is dedicated to addressing challenges in naval engineering with a forward-thinking approach, incorporating innovative technologies and current research findings. Her work aims to support the efficiency and sustainability of the maritime industry, underscoring her commitment to the field.